Hi,

You have found or be
of free copies of *Be t*
circulation around London, UK (or beyond).

If you take this copy with you, I kindly request that you:

1. **RECORD** - take a photo to let me know it has been found and who has it now. You can post it on social media and tag me **@sharmaymitchell** or sending me a message via my website (████ below).
2. **READ** it.
3. **REVIEW** it on Amazon.

4. **RE-HOME** - pass it on to someone else you think will enjoy this book to repeat the above steps.

I have faith this will work - I have faith in YOU!

Thank you,

Sharmay :)

www.sharmaymitchell.com

001

be the Uplifter

WRITTEN & ILLUSTRATED BY
SHARMAY MITCHELL

THIS IS A FREE COPY
NOT FOR SALE

READ
REVIEW (on Amazon)
RE-HOME

This poetry collection is dedicated to all the people
who have ever showed up to be my uplifter.
Thank you.

xxx

There is more of you
in the cutting of the knife
than the relenting of the bread.

CONTENTS

tightrope

818

Thin rope pulled taut,
I walk across.
If I should fall,
chalk up the loss.
My grip secure,
size up dimensions.
No slack to give,
steady through tension.

I balance with poise.
I clumsily trip.
Regain composure,
before I slip.
Some days I'm reckless.
Some days I'm careful.
A million steps,
and still I'm fearful.

I shuffle slow,
silhouette in sun.
Or sometimes fast,
the gauntlet I run.
Precariously teetering
'tween peace and strife,
I walk this tightrope
I call life.

grounding

992

I went to the tree.

I took off my boots.

I stood in the soil

to feel its gnarled roots.

I centred myself.

I felt whole and grounded.

I looked for my balance.

In nature, I found it.

eyes to the sky

741
We crouched under a blanket of darkness,

shivering in the chill.

Huddling closer for warmth,

preserving silence, mannequin still.

At first, just a few specks

announced their presence, bright.

But patience gave way to brilliance,

a billion orbs of white light.

And how thankful we were

that we had stayed longer,

stifled whimpers of trepidation,

that our faith in the wait was stronger.

And how thankful we were

that eyes could adjust.

If we never saw that beauty,

would we ever place our trust

in the existence of a higher power

that could make such wonders real?

Put these stars in our sky,

melt our hearts of steel.

I know you want to close your eyes.

I know you are tired of holding your head high.

But just look what majesty awaits

when you keep your eyes to the sky.

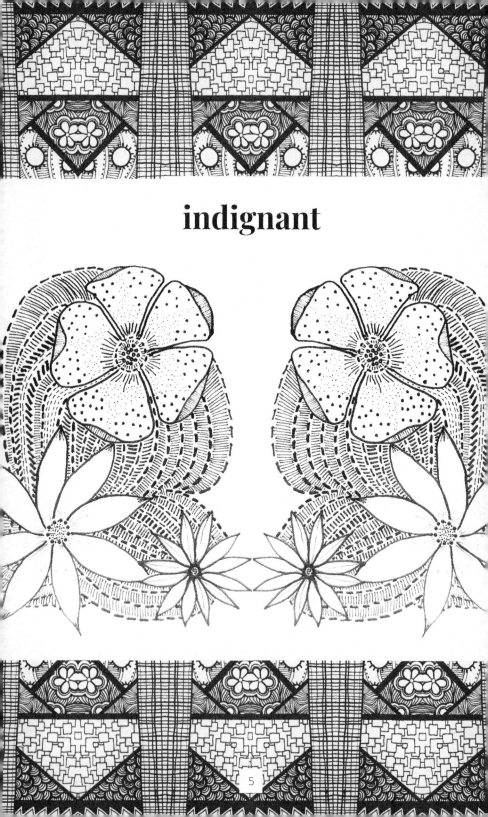

indignant

--

She hated being told that she couldn't do *it*.

Even if *it* had never before
aimlessly meandered the periphery of her vast imagination.
Even if she secretly doubted that she was capable,
the idea, that someone else had the temerity to hold a
mirror up to that ambivalence made her jaw tighten.

Underestimation was the catalyst igniting an indignant fire
inside her.
And *it* was suddenly jettisoned right into the whitest part of
the flames,
from the outer limits of nowhere,
right into the centre of her everything.

Of course, she could do *it*.

In fact,

she could do anything.

still

standing

261
Breeze never made me quiver.

In sun's glare I did not wither.

Still standing.

Standing, still.

i will

702
Thanks for the words of warning,

but I'm immune to impossibilities.

I got plenty no-can-dos

trodden into the soles of my shoes.

Naysayers are anathema.

"You can't..."

"You won't..."

"You shouldn't..."

But I will.

I will.

I will.

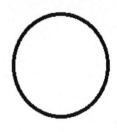

the best is yet to come

103

When mischief came to find me,
disguised as harmless fun,
I bet you wouldn't believe
how many times I've had to run.

Vaulting over skyscrapers,
for the chance to touch the sun,
I bet you wouldn't believe
the crazy things I've gone and done.

Of all the things I've seen,
all the battles I've fought and won,
I bet you wouldn't believe that, still,
the best is yet to come.

winner

207

In order to be who you are today,

did you have to bend or break?

Did you sometimes crumble under pressure,

when it was all too much to take?

Did you wake up early?

Stay up late?

Progress to pro from beginner?

Then you should take it easy on yourself,

'cos you my friend are a winner.

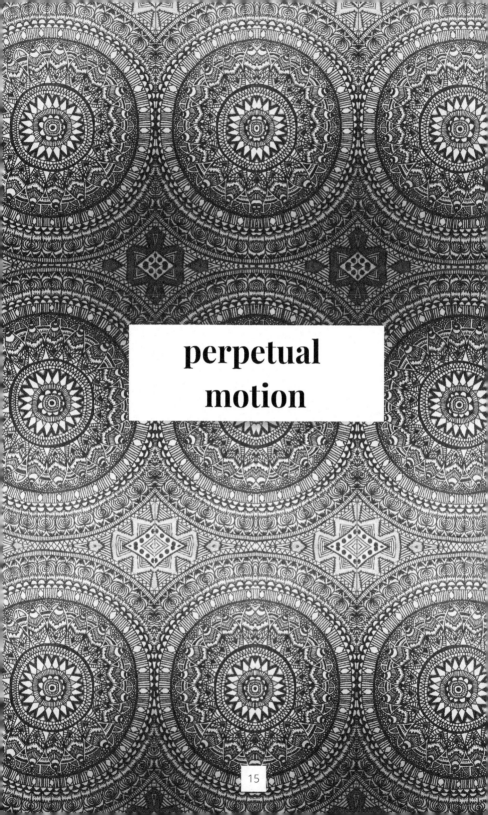

perpetual
motion

859b
With that thing gaining at your back,

dig deep and kick your heels.

The terror becomes the whip that cracks,

and legs make like they're wheels.

As energy wanes you fear the worst,

your resilience markedly thinned.

But from some place your zest is nursed,

and you find your second wind.

in storms

231

Sometimes I carry the ocean in me

and when a storm brews

my tongue makes like the crest of a wave, before it does
break,

and I can give, just as much, if not more than I take.

optimism

257
Uncertainty may billow your sails

and steer your ship on a course that will only strike land

when chance meets destiny.

But resolutely, you still stand at the bow,

deflecting trepidation,

with an unshakeable force field of optimistic calm.

when
modesty
is violence

263
Selling yourself short.

Diluting your magic.

Glass half-emptying yourself

with words like 'just' and 'only'.

Downplaying your finish as matte,

when clearly you are gloss.

Dodging superlatives

and peeling off the ones that stick.

You're a glockenspiel,

but you pretend to be a xylophone.

A Canon camera

claiming to be Fisher Price.

All so unnecessary,

let your light shine.

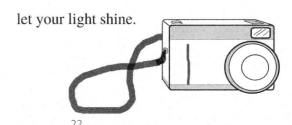

new beginnings

268
Sometimes the end is a mild poison;

a bitter pill of gnarly thorns.

Weakens you without killing,

to strengthen you for the new beginning.

inner voice

358
That voice that commands you not to stop

when the hard times get to going.

Pulls you through when muscles ache,

and lactic acid starts flowing.

You contemplate ignoring it,

but with a volume ever-growing,

there is no hiding place to cower,

from the voice all-seeing, all-knowing.

fierce

699

There is more of you

in the cutting of the knife

than the relenting of the bread.

Much more of you

in the fearless dissenter,

than the words left unsaid.

countering
with
compassion

436
Be gentle,

even with the ones who hurt you.

There is something in this world that they cradle softly

when they are not hurting you.

And that something loves them back with a passionate ferocity.

You see,

even the most diabolical can be tempered by the sweetness of love.

So,

tenderly smother them with kindness

to peel back the layers of their armour.

A fire is best fought with water.

home

460

Of all the wondrous places I've been

and all the beautiful sights I've seen,

there is no place I'd rather be

than one that accommodates you and me.

friend

902

Friend,

just your smile when I need it most,

is monsoon to hungry floodplain.

Your tender words, soft,

incapable of malice.

I don't have another you in stock

and so I feel afraid

to let you wander unattended

with strangers who may be careless with you.

You are porcelain doll;

they could break you.

And I will want to crush them.

What if they misinterpret your special for mediocre?

Manhandle your reputation?

Happiness evades me if you are sad

because you are the best friend I've ever had.

gratitude

509
Every part of this sky is magic.

It lives. It breathes. It dances.

Yet underneath it,

you spend your life fretting over ugly stressors.

Just look up and see the magnificence;

you live in a beautiful world.

butterfly
yourself

517

There is serenity in the acceptance of where you are,

but the myopic mind can breed stagnation.

If you cannot imagine anything greater than your now,

you rejoice in the chrysalis,

never touching self actualisation.

The first change is never the last.

Butterfly yourself.

transformation

526

She said goodbye.

Shed her leaves.

Stripped her bark.

Got used to the exposed feeling of naked branches.

And accepted with a sigh,

I may not look so good now,

but come spring,

I will be alright.

self-love

1291

Figuring out new ways to avoid hating yourself:

a game you wish you never had to learn to play,

but find yourself getting tangled up in every morning.

The mirror showdown,

where you plant yourself for extreme exposure therapy.

Maybe if you look long enough you might start to love what you
see?

Or, just attempt to sprint by without acknowledging the existence
of a reflection.

Maybe if you can't see yourself, the wheels and cogs of the
negative machine won't get enough steam to turn against you.

One day you won't need these games

and mirrors won't boss you.

You and the self-love will be so well acquainted,

you'll laugh about your previous sheepishness in each others'
presence.

And then you'll know what it is to love.

you made it

628
To those who leapt over the scythe

when it took a low swipe,

Achilles tendon right as rain.

And to those who limboed under the sickle,

whipping wild,

necks unsevered.

You made it.

You made it.

change
direction

45

668

Yesterday,

maybe it didn't work out.

But today is brand new.

If you have to,

take some time to stop.

Let proverbial pennies drop.

Remove blinkers.

Change direction.

Do something differently.

Because today is your now,

and now is as good a time as any.

plough on

676
Every day,

something is plotting

to murder my happiness.

And not even in solitude,

can I escape this invisible assailant.

But every day,

by sheer will and might,

I walk out of the gloom,

and into the light.

Meet it head on with vigour,

like a locomotive train,

ploughing through a foreboding mist,

and my happiness plays safe again.

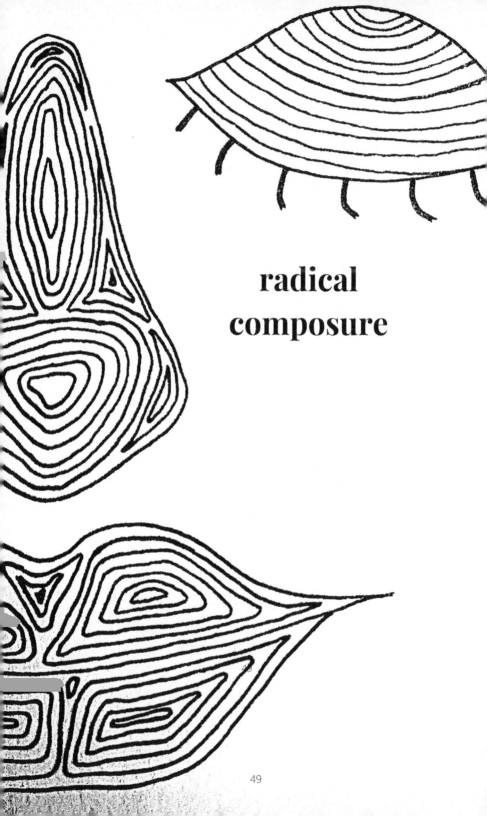

radical
composure

--

She became accustomed to withstanding

the many ways they tried to shatter her into a million pieces.

But their blows of derision and passive aggression

only stung her lightly.

And her seemingly effortless refusal

to break, bend or bow,

infused them with fury.

With a wry smile   she won.

With a cool exhale   she won.

With a nonchalant shrug   she won.

By remaining composed,

she won

again and again.

the things you are missing

1287

To see life through your fingertips
to feel its fullness and run over the jagged
points of its unforgiving parts.

To move your hands over the surface of small
things
to learn the grandeur of their worth.

To plant your back firmly against walls to feel
the room.

To judge atmosphere by breathing in the air
for the taste of humidity and pressure.

To get down low and inhale the stability of
the ground.
To roll it at the back of the throat and know
the earth does not give in.

To stand in stillness and let vibrations dance
around you.

To listen intently for the myriad of soft
sounds that would otherwise die unheard.

You have to close your eyes to see all the
things you are missing.

hope

710
In the event of the extraction of hope,

throw yourself into the fire.

When all seems lost,

scald the weakness that left you vulnerable.

Regenerate a resilience from within

to coax back the optimism

that allowed hope to flourish before.

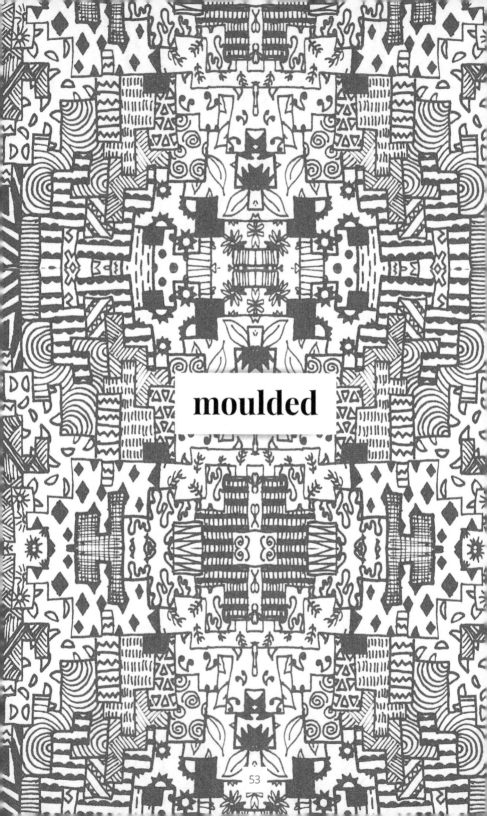

moulded

808

I've already been through the fire,

I am the fully moulded clay.

Did my time in the kiln,

and now I'm set in my ways.

There is nothing else you can show me,

that the fire did not sear into my skin,

that the heat did not coax out of my pores,

that I didn't smoke out from within.

So you must recognize I don't do compromise,

and 'no' has become my favourite word.

That fire, it burnt out the submission in me,

so now being expected to yield sounds absurd.

**everything
will fall into place**

811

In quiet cul-de-sacs,

when the mind slowed

to the thick consistency of honey,

she'd pat the ground for that thing;

that part of herself she'd thrown into the air.

A sliver of silver that missed her palm

and fluttered back into the open arms of the earth instead.

Mist made the most of a game of hide and seek,

but truly she never felt the gravity of a loss

because she knew the absence made space

for a necessary realignment within,

and that the thing she'd thrown up into the air

would always find its way home,

eventually.

she
blossomed

746
Already rooted in her convictions,

she thought it appropriate to plant herself.

And with very little nurturing at all,

she blossomed.

flaunt

835
Some people placed index finger to their lips.

Implored you to quieten your magnificence.

But in spectacular fashion, you refused.

Flaunted every inch of your flamboyance.

Poured out your vivacious energy.

Made a visual statement that

your shine

could never

be dulled.

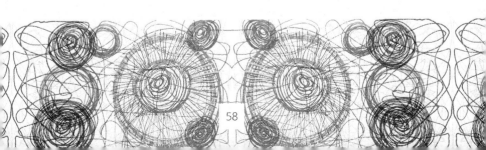

tropical downpour

850

With a Hawaiian hibiscus flower propped behind my right ear,

I can better hear the glory of the world.

The way the rain leaves nothing untouched,

birthing a symphony of purging.

Blood pressure drops as

the scent of tropical humidity fills senses with summer deluge detoxification.

Flying ants airborne,

I can spend hours lazily listening

to the way heavy droplets do a hit and run

on corrugated iron rooves, long battered by the sun.

They pour over me without remorse.

Soak my clothes, drenched.

Penetrate my scantily-clad thoughts.

And I never run for cover

because the immersion feels like

everything I ever needed,

but never knew I could have.

It washes me clean.

Sees me for who I am.

golden

1255
I'm a little bit golden,

mostly around the edges.

But on days when the sun hits my skin just right,

and I walk beneath the trees for a smattering of dappled light,

I become the grand treasure trove.

Yes.

Flecks of regality streak from my pores,

and if close enough, they reach out for yours.

By process of osmosis, you absorb some of my golden,

and realise it has the power to uplift and embolden.

metamorphosis

920

I shed my old skin on the jagged rocks.

Took the best part of a fortnight to tease it off,

peel myself out of myself.

Days of caterpillar undulation,

my smooth against the rough, and the old

eventually gave way to the new freedom.

At first,

I cowered in my nakedness,

a new me, untainted and untested.

But on the third day,

my tender skin touched the sun

and all the struggle of metamorphosis was realised.

perseverance

936
in the dark
by random grab
the best of life
you try to nab
though it may not
be what you planned
the future lies
within your hands
but if you can't
reach what you need
among the stars
you must proceed
until you find
what you desire
just persevere
and never tire

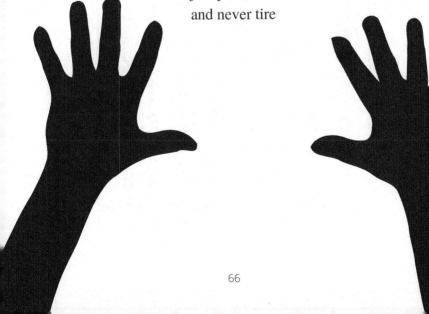

believe in yourself

1104
Spending too much time

living in the prison of other people's minds,

you'll never meet the beauty of who you truly are.

But if you believe in yourself,

champion the worth of your own wealth,

you'll unlock levels of self-love to take you far.

rhythm of life

1195

Finger on the pulse feels beat of life's rhythm.

Patience with time is the value of love given.

Permanent, physical roof over head,

makes sleep sound and safe the bed.

Hands planting seeds with hope for the growing.

Open is the mind that longs for the knowing.

If one could decipher hearts as music sheet is read.

more compassion would show in words that are said.

survival of the fittest

1301

Do you remember that time you came to sink my ship?
Rammed me starboard, and I started taking on water fast?
But I had a life raft you didn't know about
so I survived a week floating in the ocean,
catching rainwater in a plastic cup.
In my rage, I recited every wrong you had ever committed
against me.
Dolphins heard, took pity and brought me sushi.
You came back and found me beating the odds
so you punctured my raft,
and I was left floating on its deflated carcass.
With no more cup and dolphins long gone,
I was on the brink of death
until the winds picked up in my favour.
Blew me to an unknown, but inhabited, archipelago,
where the indigenous people hauled me onto dry land,
nursed me back to full strength.
You did everything you could to end me
and yet still, I'm here.

just fine

1099
this is but a pinch of salt

in the vast sea of time

you are a long way from saturation

you will be just fine

Scan this QR code for updates on the author's next projects

About the author

Sharmay Mitchell is a born and raised west-Londoner who values being creative as an active part of maintaining mental wellness. For over 3 years, she created one new artistic piece each day and became known as "that girl who writes a poem a day". The number before each poem in this book represents the day on which it was written.

In 2020, she performed a poem for the Notting Hill Carnival virtual event. In 2019, her poetry was published in the Words by__ anthology, fundraising for UNICEF. And in 2018, one of her poems placed third in the London Loop Writing Competition. Her jewellery has been featured in productions by actor, writer and producer, Issa Rae and, most impressively, she has won critical acclaim amongst scores of under-5s for her puppet show performances, face painting and juggling skills.

She loves symmetry, intricate patterns, cats, playing made-up ditties on her mbira, the scent of lavender, eating soursop, Julie mangoes and plantain, cutting into perfectly ripened avocados, giving people gifts and sunny summer days. She is currently working on a couple of children's books and an initiative to uplift Londoners through positive messages around the city- an extension of **be the Uplifter**.

Sharmay's message:
"If I'd never challenged myself to create something new every day, none of the illustrations or poems in this book would exist. I hope you enjoyed reading them, and if you did, I'd be eternally grateful if you would:
- leave a review on Amazon.
-follow me on my Instagram account @sharmaymitchell
-be the uplifter and gift this book to your friends, family, work colleagues, or someone who you think needs some uplifting words."

www.sharmaymitchell.com

THIS IS A FREE COPY
NOT FOR SALE

Printed in Great Britain
by Amazon

28836616R00051